LET THERE BE
Light

The Lumination of Nia

SONYA CAROL THOMAS

ISBN 979-8-88616-366-7 (paperback)
ISBN 979-8-88616-367-4 (digital)

Copyright © 2022 by Sonya Carol Thomas

All rights reserved. No part of this publication may be reproduced, distributed, or transmitted in any form or by any means, including photocopying, recording, or other electronic or mechanical methods without the prior written permission of the publisher. For permission requests, solicit the publisher via the address below.

Christian Faith Publishing
832 Park Avenue
Meadville, PA 16335
www.christianfaithpublishing.com

Printed in the United States of America

CONTENTS

Foreword v
Introduction vii

Foundation 1
   Spiritual Foundation 2
   Rituals 4
   Cultural Intelligence 5
   Learning Styles 5
Pathway 12
   Readiness 12
   Speed 14
   Motivation 15
   Know-How 16
   Diligence 18
Heart's Desire 21
Center Point 24
   Vision 24
   Purpose 25
Razor's Edge 28
Centrifugal Force: The Science of Nia 30
Star Points 32
   A Star 32
   Anchor 35
   Peer 38
   Mentor 39
   Sponsorship 44
   Champion 46

Distractions 50
Give and Receive 55

References 59

FOREWORD

Foreword by:
Nanette M. DePriest, NIA Star Concept
Coworker, Associate, Friend

It was truly a blessing to meet and work with Dr. Sonya Thomas for many years. Her career achievements matched with personal accomplishments are a living example of the Nia Star concept that I shaped with the intent to drive success of personal vision. Today, as I write this foreword for her captivating memoir, I am humbled by the depth of knowledge and wisdom shaping a commentary that enhances the concept with encouragement for personal confidence in a variety of facets of life.

The illumination of intelligence on the pages to follow prompts inspiration to establish a firm vision. There is bright insight in this book with pivotal points to understand indelible values that builds fortitude and stamina of personal pathways fueled with purposeful collective power for motivative action to achieve goals. Literacy gained for personal growth from the wisdom shared is like the magnitude of stars, so **_Let There Be Light._**

Dr. Sonya C. Thomas, author
Author of **Reasons of Love**
Executive Director of The John Maxwell Team
Founder and President of George Thomas Coaching, Consulting, and Training Growth Services, LLC,
www.gtgrowthservices.com

INTRODUCTION

The framework I am about to present to you is so simplistic that you will wonder why you had not thought of it before. It is so common in a sense that as we pick nuggets of life from others, we never think about bucketizing these nuggets, neither do we think on who gave them to us in such a way. We can follow the path as to who God intended for us to be. Instead, we trudge along, attempting to make life happen on our own, especially after we reach "adulthood" and leave (move) from "Mama and Daddy's" house. Oh yeah, we know it all. Along the journey, we fail, but we get back up, picking up a few thistles and thorns. Somehow, we gather enough flowers to make a bouquet, but it may not be enough flowers to make a garden or at least not to our satisfaction based on our definition of success.

In the journey of life, there are inherent and instinctive positive possibilities. I would be cruel and discouraging to you by having you think that all of life's journey are negative. If we look at it with our lenses, we will capture many life lessons on our journey; it is full of lessons we can learn from. If you stimulate your mind into looking at the structure of going through your journey, you will understand the opportunities for expanded growth in every area of your life—socially, culturally, educationally, charitability, spiritually, physically, etc. You get the picture?

This framework requires you to understand your purpose, your calling, and your reason that you are on earth. If you have not discovered your purpose, let me take you through a course. Once you discover your purpose, you will sense peace on everything you do every day. In actuality, you will look for ways to walk in your purpose—daily. Aren't you frustrated with working the job you do not like? Are you ready to let the adventure begin? What about feeling like you have no direction? Are you ready to live your best? Live on purpose. Well, you cannot do it alone. Join me as we wish upon the star of success—the Nia Star Concept. Nia Star will take you to your sweet spot, and best of all, you have others joining, helping, cheering, and directing you through your beautiful boulevard of life. Let your little light shine. Uncover, discover, and explore the illumination of Nia—your purpose, your star, your Nia.

FOUNDATION

Getting an understanding of who you are, what makes you you, and looking at how you got here

We all are different—UNIQUE! Just like stars in the sky. On a clear night, when you look up at the sky, you see a plethora of stars. Amazingly, not one is the same. That is the same with you, even if you are a twin. We are different. That uniqueness was shaped in your mother's womb (Jeremiah 1:5). Upon your birth, your uniqueness began to write its own story. There are impactful experiences that shape memories. You have the environment to thank for those experiences you have been exposed to as well as people, places, and things you have seen.

I remember as far back as locking myself in the bathroom when I was two years old. My two brothers and I went to visit our maternal grandparents. I had to go to the bathroom. Now this was public housing in the early sixties. The door was heavy with a glass visor above that opened for ventilation. The doorknob was a brass heavy knob with a turnable (tumble) latch. For some reason, I felt the need to keep brothers Victor and Kevin out because they were boys. I understood gender difference already. So I turned the latch to lock the door.

After I used the toilet and washed my hands, I went to open the door. Oh boy, I forgot how to turn the latch. I could not figure out how to unlock the door. I cried out for my brothers. They could not open the door from the outside. They were no help. I cried harder. My grandparents came to give me instructions. I was too confused and upset to follow any instructions. Grandma called upon her pastor and his wife, who lived in the building, to help. The pastor got a ladder to look over into the bathroom visor. He comforted me and provided instructions. Luckily, because it was summertime, the visor was open. The pastor's wife directed my hands to the doorknob then to the latch.

"Turn it, baby," she said. I did, and I opened the door. I ran out into Grandma's arms. This story has been with me for over sixty years.

After reaching adulthood, whenever I went to my grandmother's church, the question was asked ALWAYS. "Is this the grandbaby who locked herself in the bathroom?"

"I am her," I would answer. That experience exposed me to following directions and noticing latch locks on older doors. I am very mindful and understanding how to get out of a stall or room once I am inside. Can you reflect back to a situation that marked and raised your awareness of your surroundings?

That story was an experience for an innocent little girl. But what about experiences that lead you down different roads? We have many. I know I do. Those experience generally have connections attached to them. Connection of people, connections to places, or connections to things. Very seldom do we do things alone or in a vacuum. However, the values are instilled in you that shape and make you into your unique self. In your value system comes a spiritual foundation, emotional intelligence, cultural intelligence, learning styles, physical capabilities, beliefs, drive, and habits. This value system is the total sum of who you are and helps establish a path to how you pursue and establish goals.

Spiritual Foundation

Your spiritual foundation incorporates so many aspects of your beliefs, culture, and even rituals. Let us focus on just the spiritual aspect of the foundation.

LET THERE BE LIGHT

There is an order of who is who. What I mean, the child sees parents as supreme. However, once the child understands words and directions, the child is usually taught about a higher power that directs and controls the entire world—God. But if we look at it closer, children have imagination to understand God is a spirit. Your faith in God's existence was very easy to establish. From there, you learned other aspects of God—the Ten Commandments, the Beatitudes, Psalm 23, the Lord's Prayer, and of course, Jesus Christ, if the teaching is of Christianity. Best of all, your spiritual foundation includes going to heaven if we do good and love one another. Of course, there is more to it than that, but you get the point.

As we get older, our foundation shows areas of attending worship services on our Sabbath day—Friday if Jewish, Saturday if Seventh Day Adventist, and Sunday if Protestant or Catholic. As a little girl, I remember getting dressed up then in a dress, ruffle socks, hat, and gloves—sharp—to go to church. Everyone in the neighborhood went to church, except the bad people (the unsaved). Praying before bed was common and so was praying before every meal.

I like what I read somewhere on the internet: "A foundation is the load-bearing part of a building (Your life) and is below ground"—it cannot be seen. This means that your spiritual foundation, too, is what holds you strong, especially during tough times. The mere fact that your spiritual foundation cannot be seen says a lot about how you carry out your day to day, among other things.

Your spiritual foundation must be stronger and deeper than those around you. Weak spiritual foundation will develop cracks and will soon collapse, not only spiritually, but emotional. That may show up in the physical (nervous breakdown, psychological problem, mental issues, etc.). A spiritual weakness shows negative signs that impact others such as bad attitudes, lack of commitment, fear/doubt, offensive and offenses, conflicts, lack of control, even jealously…in other words, the lust of the flesh (Galatians 5:23).

Building a strong secure spiritual foundation means you are standing securely, firmly, and confidently on what and who you say you believe and trust in—for me, it is Jesus Christ, my Savior. That spiritual foundation keeps me praying, meditating, and worshipping Him. It keeps me to love Him and His people—that is EVERYONE. It keeps me in walking and seeking all truth for my life. What is your spiritual foundation looking like? Who is your Supreme Being? How strong do you trust in your God? Have you established a spiritual foundation? Unsurprisingly, wishing upon this star and discovering and walking in your purpose requires a strong, secure, and firm spiritual foundation. Afterall, He created you and is the reason behind your existence here on this planet.

As you dive deeper into your spiritual foundation, you can see how manners and courtesy play a part. What is your behavior like toward others? Are you polite or rude? Of course, with a strong spiritual foundation, you would not dare display rude behavior, or would you? Mama said, "Manners are free. Be courteous to everyone." That is a part of my spiritual foundation.

Rituals

Rituals are illogic and irrational to those on the outside of your circle. It is thought to be a formalism, traditionalism of systematic behaviors. Here is a clear example. I taught a class titled intercultural communication in the local college. I enjoyed the lesson on rituals and beliefs. There are many rituals that we carry through in our lives that we believe; it is how everyone does it. It is amazing how families celebrate (or not) holidays—even how birthdays are celebrated. In a world of vast diversity, it is delightful to learn different ways to celebrate our smallest ritual.

One ritual that I have noticed is the first day of school. Back when I went to school, it was not a big deal. Well, now it is. Children are photographed with their backpack, new cute outfits or uniforms, and a big smile. Some include a chalkboard poster "First grade—here comes Sonya." This ritual journey continues annually until the first day of twelfth grade.

Our rituals are a part of our foundation and are carried through in aspects of our lives. Rituals give us a place of pride and fulfillment as self-actualization and belongingness in our culture (Maslow 1943).

Cultural Intelligence

Culture is infused with values, traditions, rituals, and spiritual foundation because of how they all are intertwined. Culture is the guidelines for dress, behavior, social norms, and language. There are customary beliefs and social norms which are shared within our families and groups. What you do in your group/family may look so odd from an outsider's perspective. How you dress may not be acceptable in another's culture. Culture is a learned behavior and has its place along the Nia Star since culture is a guiding compass of our behavior.

Let's look at gender for example. In some cultures, toys are assigned to boys or girls (trucks or dolls). There has been a great embracing of gender dominate vocation also. I worked in a male-dominating field as an electric field technician. Not only did I work outside, but I put my hands on the electric meter and its inner parts. If the problem was not at the meter, I went inside to the disconnect panel to make minor repairs. Boy, did I get stares of doubt and concerns about me working in a man's field from customers. Culturally, our sociality is breaking barriers of culture dominance. Our society is breaking some of these cultural strongholds.

There are still flaws in sexual orientation because of our own beliefs and culture. Nonetheless, culture plays an integral part in your foundation. Remember, we are about what makes you—YOU.

Learning Styles

There are four different learning styles: visual, audio, reading/writing, and kinesthetic. This is another component that makes us different. We apply to our natural-born canvas differently. We all receive and process information differently. I for one learn by inquiry—as I receive information, my mind goes into an inquisitive mode. I ask many questions, period. I notice some of my teachers would become a bit irritated because of this. As I got older, I learned to frame my questions differently as to not frustrate the one I am getting the information from. You know, it may seem a bit intimidating. I understand that, but that is not my intention.

To show I am an engaged learner to the information being given me, I process information by turning words into picture—into puzzle pieces. I imagine pulling the pieces apart and putting them back together. For example, when hearing a story from the Bible, I envision every scene, every color, the surroundings, the crowd, the woman pressing her way to touch the hem of Jesus's garment, and, virtually, being released from Jesus to the woman. Although virtual is intangible, in my mind I have to make it tangible. Another example is the process of germination—the tilling, the weeding, the planting, the watering, and the seeding. My mind processes each step with a question, "Why is this happening?" "How is it happening?" "What is happening?"

These questions aid in me learning and understanding. The kind of learner I am, according to Flemings (1987) in the VARK model is a kinesthetic learner. The VARK model has four learning styles—visual, audio, reading/writing, and kinesthetic.

Another topic on learning styles would be Multiple Intelligence (Gardner 1999). There are eight multiple intelligences: linguistic, logical/mathematical, spatial, kinesthetic, interpersonal, intrapersonal, musical, and naturalistic. Garner contends how we all learn and process by our different skill sets that we were born with. We are skilled at one of these intelligences. You do not process only one way; you may be efficient in more than one of these intelligences.

What I like about multiple intelligences is the emphasis that we are all *smart* in our God-given talent. I am not gifted in art, I cannot sing, I cannot draw, or create anything artistic although I can sew, crochet, and knit. It is because I can follow a pattern; my linguistic and logical intelligences are strong. When you think about your learning style, the one you learn best, you have found your sweet spot of learning and applying what you have learned. Ask yourself, what style or class or classes did you flourish in? PE, arts and crafts, music, English, etc.?

I also like how the multiple intelligences include everyone with their own unique value to learning and processing knowledge. Linguistic learners learn and apply reading strategies and even explore creative written words. I remember enjoying an English class called creative writing. In this class, we had assignments of interpreting writing poetry and writing imagination story. My favorite was to update a children story to modern times.

Are you one who gravitates toward linguistics and listening? You may gravitate to speeches, speaking in front of audiences, writing prose of various types, or reading books. You may have a strong linguistic intelligence. In conjunction, those who love numbers, pose and test hypothesis, and think mathematical patterns—a game such as calculating, algorithm and statistics, and technology and science—have a strong logical and mathematical learning intelligence.

Those who can visually and physically move their body parts or use 3D imagery have a kinesthetic and spatial intelligence. Until I learned about multiple intelligences, I did not understand how dancers or athletes improve their craft. One day, I was watching a sports show on television. The host was explaining the science in the athlete's body movement—as in the angles and position a baseball player stands to hit a fastball. The host explained in slow motion how a basketball player makes dunk shots. I was impressed how much motion must be delivered before the player leaps off his feet to dunk. And how, at the right angle and with the right force, a baseball player swings to hit the ball and sends it over and out of the park. This was kinesthetic intelligence in action. Many times, athletes review a video over and over, capturing what went right and what was wrong in the execution to make improvements.

A dancer can move his or her body with ease that flows to music, which tells a story. Those with kinesthetic intelligence have developed a sense of coordination and timing. You and I may call this person a natural.

Known as the mother of American modernism, American artist, Georgia O'Keeffe, said, "I found that I could say things with color and shape that I had no words for." That is exactly what strong visual/spatial intelligence is. This type of person learns best by seeing and observing and seeing it in 3D. Spatial is understanding how one's body is in relationship to space. We use visual/spatial in driving and navigating from place to place. Even flowing in traffic requires special visual. So then, who are strong in this intelligence?

Spatial intelligence has the ability to transform objects to mental rotation. Many kinesthetic intelligences also are strong spatial learners. Are you understanding why you like or dislike building blocks, jigsaw puzzles, or reading maps? It is not your inability to learn it as much as it is not your strongest intelligence.

I love Stevie Wonder. I proclaimed him as my husband when I was four, and he was 11. We just never met up. Nonetheless, I love his music; I love his artistry. Stevie can take any conversation and turn it into a song right on the spot. That is musical intelligence at its finest. Remember "Fingertips—Part 1 and 2"? Stevie played his harmonica to the tune of "Mary Had a Little Lamb." As children, we all have sung that song. How does that relate to musical intelligence, you may wonder.

One with musical intelligence has an ability to strongly recognize, create, produce, and reflect on music. They genuinely have sensitive ears to melodic sounds. In "Fingertips—Part 1 and 2," I only imagined that Stevie heard "Mary Had a Little Lamb" in the beat and tone as we clapped and shouted "Yeah!" He had to give us the sample. As many times I have seen Stevie in concert, he has shown his amazing musical intelligence.

Another multiple intelligence is that of interpersonal. One would think an interpersonal intelligence is the strongest intelligence, but it is not as strong as many people think. Interpersonal intelligence enables us to understand and communicate with others, with sensitivity to differences in moods, temperaments, and motivations. Those with interpersonal intelligence develops relationships fairly easy and looks to better equality and equity to all. Of course, building relationships are not self-serving but for a positive development of society and the community.

Power is a word deep from our core of understanding ourselves, of our thoughts and feelings. The more we understand ourselves, the sooner we can relate to the outer world. However, the intrapersonal intelligence has a keen sense of self and pretty much all around us. Those with a strong intrapersonal intelligent quality tend to work well independently and are very self-directed. They are aware of their emotions and seek to finding their life's purpose and self-actualization. Have you found yourself in deep thought, almost in a trance? Are you thinking about your goals, and do you express yourself by journaling?

Journaling is a daunting chore to some but a blessed outlet for the intrapersonal intelligent person. That is one way that inner thoughts are displayed to the outer world. Do not mistake those in this intelligence for being shy. For example, First Lady Eleanor Roosevelt was considered as having intrapersonal intelligence but was definitely not shy.

A naturalist intelligence "is one who is able to recognize flora and fauna to make consequential distinction in the natural world and to use this ability productive in hunting and farming and biological science" (Gardner 1995). The skill of a naturalistic person works well with plants and animals. The inquisitive mind of George Washington Carver led him into the many uses of a peanut. In such, those with a naturalistic wonder and curiosity causes new uncovered phenomena of life. I recall playing with my neighbor Donna. She and I played in dirt, making mud pies. After her family moved, I did not make mud pies again. I did not put my hands in dirt again until forty years later. When Richard and I moved to Auburn Hills, I felt compelled to do it again—to put my hands in dirt. I found how much fun and relaxing it is to be so close to nature, the earth, the sun, the birds, the trees, and the wind. That is as close to using my naturalistic intelligence as I can get.

These are some careers that align with the different intelligences.

1. **Verbal/linguistic:** writers, authors, speakers, four times, broadcasters, attorney, counselors, teachers, readers, and researchers
2. **Logical/mathematical:** computer technology, law, accountant, economist, financier, engineer, chemist, medical doctor, scientist, and detective
3. **Tactile-Kinesthetic:** actor, actress, dancer, athlete, seamstress, tailor, model, surgeon, builder
4. **Visual/Spatial:** architect, mechanical engineer, artist, photographer, designer, pilot, art critic, hair stylist, makeup artist, forensic, and daydreamers
5. **Musical:** singer, instrumentalist, sound engineer, producer, credit, instrument maker, teacher, and conductor
6. **Interpersonal:** teaching, social work, counseling, management drama politics, and actor
7. **Intrapersonal:** self-directed assignments, researcher, computer programmers, spiritual leaders, philosophers, and psychologist
8. **Naturalist:** biologist, ecologist, chemistry, zoologist, forestry, and botanist

Your Reflection Toolkit

1. As you reflect on your upbringing, what were the rituals and traditions that you depended on?
2. If you no longer honor or celebrate old family traditions and rituals, why? Did you replace them? If so, with what and why?
3. Reflect back on coming into your faith (or no faith practice).
4. Culture are those beliefs that guide our day-to-day behaviors. Describe your cultural intelligence.

5. Take a learning style assessment. Go to the link http://www.educationplanner.org/students/self-assessments/learning-styles.shtml.

PATHWAY

How to determine and affirm readiness to step forward—what you got to work with

Now that you understand the formation of your foundation, it is time to look at your pathway—your direction, your movement to getting to where your dream is—that beautiful boulevard. The pathway can be seen in six components: readiness, speed, motivation, know-how, diligence, and confidence. As you set out through your pathway, you must see yourself moving. Standing still does not get you to a new place. Yes, there may be a moment where you stand still. Standing still is for pondering, meditating, and decision-making. That is not what we are talking about here.

Readiness

As you think about pathway, begin to think on readiness—being ready for the journey. Readiness is an army term but can be used for civilian. Often, a person wants the dream but concludes that the timing is not right; he concludes that it is not to be. Even so, one may not be ready for the tasks that is required. According to *Merriam-Webster*, *readiness* is the state of being fully prepared for something, even the willingness to do something (2020). Only you can answer the questions regarding your own readiness. You must examine your physical, mental, emotional, and spiritual state of being for ready.

Let us think about becoming a yoga instructor. A yoga instructor requires preparation—physically, emotionally, mentally, and, yes, spiritually. Physically, a yogi must develop the stamina to go through the physical. Yoga instructor Nakia Reeves explained that one must be emotionally ready for the changes the "lifestyle" of a yoga requires. In conjunction with emotional, one must be mentally ready for the embracement of the yoga lifestyle. She further explained that yoga teaching is a philosophy which aligns with a commitment of being good to earth. Nakia summed it up that spiritual embracement is to have a spiritual source which is bigger than oneself. Based on this short summary of yoga, I had to ask myself, "Am I ready for that?" I thought it was positioning my body in different postures for exercise. Boy, was I wrong! I am not ready to move in that area, at least not yet. However, I could position my mind (mental) to it once given more information on becoming ready.

Readiness of any kind (business, organizational, etc.) measures the preparedness to undergo major changes or the ability to take on new projects. In Luke 14:28–30, we learn that we should count the cost to build. This does include building on our dreams, aspirations, and inspirations. One does not dream of being a doctor without considering the schooling, the studying, and the sacrificing it requires. Your readiness—counting the cost—means recognizing and agreeing to what it takes to get to the end. This can be true in wanting a big mansion—counting the cost of cleaning and maintaining it and affording the utilities to live comfortable in the big mansion.

You may ask yourself, How do you know if you are ready? A readiness assessment like counting the cost may be helpful in knowing and understanding if you are ready. You may want to consider your project, your goals, and your objectives. You may have concerns, and you may have some expectations. Count up the cost, the support that you may need, and the ability to change and perhaps to adapt to the changes that may occur. Consider the needs, the governance, and recognize how and when to make decisions, and do not forget the potential mishaps and mistakes that may occur along the way. In counting up the cost, you want to be sure that you are ready.

Speed

How many times have we looked at microwaving food? We microwave food because we want the food hot quickly. We do not want to spend time cooking conventionally (gas oven or electric stove). Just the same, we want everything quick. Look at the commercial of JG Wentworth: "It's my money and I want it NOW!" Let's go even further.

Many times, the education process is guilty right now of the outcomes. There are accelerated degree programs which shortens the time in the program. On your pathway, you must ask yourself, What speed are you accelerating to get there? If you are driving your tactics fast or slow, what does the outcome look like? You are ready to go, but you may not want to go slow. If you are going too fast, understand crucial information may not be gained. How many signs are you blowing through going fast? What are you missing along the way? Not gaining crucial information may sabotage effectiveness of your future. Develop a moderate pace—one that allows for growth and inquiry.

I remember training for a new position. The person who was assigned to train me in the field trained me on the steps without explaining why each step had its importance. A week later, I was on my own. A month later, I turned in all my work. I was surprised to see all my work back on my desk the next day. The training was fast. Questions were not answered for me to understand each step's importance. This is what I mean about speed. Sometimes, you may need to slow down your steps so that you understand what is happening throughout the journey by using critical thinking and asking questions. Having a steady pace gives you pause to understand, analyze, and assess your expected outcome.

LET THERE BE LIGHT

Motivation

Your motivation may not be in alignment with your desire since desires, as we have learned, are in the heart, and motivation is the fuel. Desires are designed in the heart as possibilities of wants. Needless to say, desires do not mean one is motivated to work the work. Instead, high motivation fuels what one desires. Sort of like octane fuel (93) oppose to regular fuel (87).

There may be situations that shortchange, frustrate, or irritate one's desire, but does that situation cause enough irritation to influence a change where you want to be? If not, what are you going to do about it? Someone quoted "Change is going to change whether you change." How motivated are you to follow your pathway to change your position?

Being motivated means being purposeful, being intentional. Going back to school for certification or a degree has a purpose with an expected outcome. That is intentional with motivation as the driver or influencer. As you prepare to fill-in blanks of your Nia Star, understand how motivation—your motivation works contemporaneously with speed and readiness.

When there is no motivation to move forward, whether to learn, grow, or change, there is no movement. Yet, it is to say motivation is in conjunction with one's beliefs. If there is no belief that the task is possible, the motivation is diminished. Taking on the task usually does not happen. Through the change process, motivation flows with high communication of learning, smoother transitions, and decreased anxieties with increased creativity. The experience is thus joyful and exciting.

Adult learning theorist Malcolm Knowles (1989) points out that adults must know why they should learn or do something. Once learned, the adult learner will enter the learning or change environment with high motivation. Ask yourself again, "How motivated are you to make your changes, to move in your desired direction of your expected outcome—your beautiful boulevard?"

We examined the foundation and looked at who we are and why we believe the way we do, but we have not discussed what influences and motivates us from a cultural frame. What we have experienced on life's journey has roots of our cultural beliefs into what we *think* we can/cannot do or become. Because of these experiences, we can withhold or dismiss the desire within by believing that we cannot or should not pursue the desire. These lies or bogus stories have limiting beliefs of who God says we are (Ephesians 2:10) and what we can do ("I can do ALL things through Christ which strengthens me" [Philippians 4:13]) because of your gender, age, social economic status, etc.

One of the indicators of high motivation is that one will work harder, longer, and intentionally, not omitting, being open to the new adventure. Various cultural beliefs may trigger different emotions—joy, frustration, irritation, and determination. According to Wlodkowski (2008), "Emotions also give texture to events and help us to understand them."

Know-How

Krathwohl (2002) categorized knowledge in four dimensions: factual knowledge, conceptual knowledge, procedural knowledge, and metacognitive knowledge. The first dimension of knowledge is *factual knowledge*. This knowledge is where terminologies and specific details are known. To obtain factual knowledge is learned through exposure, repetition, and rote memory. Remember your spelling list from third grade? Those words were factual. You may have written them down ten times to transfer the words to your memory. If you had a teacher like me, you had to put the words in a sentence and provide the definition. Factual knowledge is like being a breathing encyclopedia. The facts are there—now what?

The second dimension of knowledge is *conceptual knowledge*. Conceptual knowledge is related to factual knowledge as knowing the interrelationships and/or functions of details that make up a larger picture. Conceptual knowledge put principles in general generalities into theories and models that help us utilize the information. You want to conceptualize differences and meaningfulness in principles in a sort of template or framework, in which you can follow. You may have heard the same: "you don't need to recreate the wheel, but you need to conceptualize the wheel's usefulness."

The third dimension is *procedural knowledge*. What I like about procedural knowledge is knowledge of subject specific skills and algorithms, techniques, and methods. In procedural knowledge, you may understand criteria in using the correct procedures. When I was a technical trainer, I made sure the trainee understood steps in performing tasks from beginning to the end. The technical tasks were developed around factual knowledge and procedural knowledge.

The fourth and final dimension is *metacognitive knowledge*. Krathwohl (2002) explained that metacognitive knowledge generally is the least recognized because we do not reflect on what is happening internally. If we reflect, we may recognize our ability to strategize. Inside of our soul, we are tossing around cognitive thoughts to make meaning of a concept.

You may ask, How do these four dimensions play into "know-how?" However, you get knowledge either explicitly—it is written down and is articulated—or implicitly, that is tasks and skills transferability from organization or department. There is also tactic knowledge, which is personal. You have experienced great things in your lifetime, even if it did not feel good during that time. Those experiences have garnered you some foundation of know-how. Now you know how to do some things, if not many things…you fill in the blank.

I think about the book *Everything I know I Learned in Kindergarten* by Robert Fulghum (2003). You have some know-how already. The mere fact you are reading this book indicates the know-how to read. Further, into examining know-how, your desires can be based on small level of what you are drawn to. For example, even developing an interest in electricity may come about from changing a light bulb or resetting a circuit breaker or playing with dolls and truck as children. Those early days of playing introduced you to dress-up, make-up, pickup, and fix it. You developed new skills for newer tasks and forms into your know-how. We gather know-how by inquiry and procedural inquisition: *What?*—facts; *Why?*—science; *Who?*—communication, street-smarts opposed to book smarts, and tactical knowledge, which is hard to transfer by means of written or verbal direction. The opposite is explicit knowledge.

As I write this section, I thought about a hairdresser named Char. Char began doing hair as an eight-year old. She did not possess factual knowledge, except in reading. She had now know-how, which is what got her into her career and her purpose is her know-how. What Char has is talent that takes her deep into her success and she works her skill with ease as a cosmetologist. She went to cosmetology school to get her license from the state. That just add to her know-how. I have watched Char work her know-how. Added with her factual, procedural, and conceptional knowledge, she is successful. Know-how is nothing without knowledge. Knowledge can only take you but so far, but know-how will take you to the end.

Diligence

Your pathway is nothing without your diligence, commitment, or requirement to maintain consistent movement. You must stay in a mobile motion. Look at it this way: as you stand in the middle of the road, you are getting nowhere standing still. The finish line is ahead of you but only is accomplished by your diligence to moving toward it. Don't stand there! Get into motion. Move! One step at a time or one bite at a time. Be diligent. First, identify all that it takes to accomplish your goal. You need research on the subject matter.

As an example, deciding to go back to school for a degree takes more than the desire. One must decide what kind of degree. Decide what kind of degree, what school or institution to apply, the cost, and the program are other factors. Once all these things are decided and selected, you must look at every course and its requirements. I did this for my education. It made every step not only intentionally, but also kept me within the purposed desire. Knowing each step kept me diligent to the goal. I could see it (the finish line). Understand that the work was as intense and challenging, but it was worth my diligence and commitment. I kept reminding myself, *If it were easy, everyone who wants this would have it.* Your pathway has a light to follow to stay diligent. Do you finish what you start? Are you a finisher and a completer? Are you looking at all the requirements it takes to reach your goal? Are you a procrastinator? Are you counting the cost? Do you give up and quit?

I was scared, especially at the beginning of the college education pursuit. I did not believe I could accomplish the goal. My self-efficacy was low. Efficacy beliefs shape individual's expectation. The source of self-efficacy comes by way of (1) mastery experiences, (2) vicarious experiences, (3) social persuasion, and (4) emotional or somatic state (Bandura 1993).

Mastery experiences requires diligence in making one's way through. You make your way through the path by your experiences and your commitment. It may seem like a spinning circle—it is. Your experience, your commitment, and your determination are all in play simultaneously.

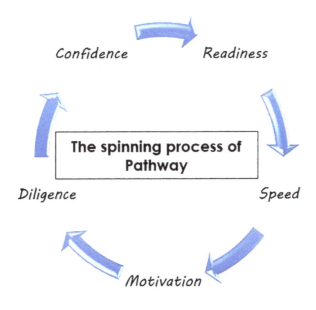

If you are not confident in your pursuit but have readiness, speed, and motivation, you can continue to move. The confidence will catch up. However, if you are confident but lack readiness, motivation, diligence, and speed, believe you me—you will not move. As a matter of fact, you are confidently standing still! You must find your place on this wheel so that you can create a strategy of movement. Whatever your pathway looked like prior to this book can change you to a steadier mobile foundation pillar. Are you ready to rescript your infrastructure so you may live your life on a beautiful boulevard? Welcome to movement. Onward! Upward!

Your Reflection Toolkit

1. How can you determine that you are ready to work out and live your purpose?
2. What are your motivations?
3. There are skills you process. How can you use them to travel your travel along your boulevard?

HEART'S DESIRE

How to be in touch with your heart's desire for life goals; feel it

Heart's desire is generally defined as something that you want very much. It comes straight from the depth of the heart. In order for us to discover our heart's desire, develop the ability to hear, we must learn and trust our heart. There are many scriptures in the Bible regarding our heart's desire and planning on executing it.

One grandmother shared her heart's desire with her granddaughter. She desired that all the grandchildren will live successful and gratifying lives and for them to make sure loved ones know they are loved. How did the grandmother discover her heart's desire, one might ask? Perhaps wisdom or experience led her to this desire. It takes making sacred space to listen to the longings, the calling, and the purpose that makes one's heart sing. This is not easy. Neither is carrying the plan for the heart's desire. You might encounter pitfalls, orange barrels, and detours. That is what life is about. It is NEVER too late to begin to traverse the path to your heart's desire.

I love hearing the stories of those who always desired to play professional football, basketball, or become an attorney, etc. Michael Jordan, for instance, desired basketball so much that he was never seen without a basketball in his hands. Your heart's desire can be one of the strongest forces (motivation) that will keep you on track when it is in alignment with your vision. Jordan saw himself playing professional basketball.

Heart's desire is given to you from above. God gives the desire to you so you can have hope of a good life. Heart's desire causes us to dream and inspire in leaving a legacy. Have you set your heart's desire on your dream? If not, you can change your perspective. Stop looking at things from that old lens, and try on a new pair of glasses. Look at how you are going to achieve what you want. This takes some strategizing, some planning, and some goal-setting. Do not compare yourself to anyone else; that can be kind of arduous. You may use someone as a model or framework instead. Each one of us has a personal path to follow. We can look over to our right and to our left, but we should not compare. Be aware of self-sabotaging. Do not be your own worst enemy; instead, be your own best friend. Exercise your goal. What I mean here is keep it moving. When it seems that you come to a snag, do not give up. Try making course corrections, but keep the gold the dream—the aspiration, the heart's desire in focus.

Do you know what triggers you to get off track? Your fears may have kept you from your heart's desire. This book is about the Nia concept. In the Nia concept, an accountability partner or buddy is essential for your success. Ask for help when you need it. And lastly, give yourself a timeline and a deadline to achieve your heart's desire. Your heart's desire will not come fast like fast-food, easy like apple pie, or quick like oatmeal. It will take time. Trust the process.

Ask yourself these questions:

1. What is my heart's deepest desire?
2. What is missing in my life?
3. What would my heart song be?
4. What do I secretly long to be, to do, or to have?
5. If I was to let myself just dream, what would I dream that I am doing?

What is getting in the way of your dream—your heart's desire? Have you been discouraged from dreaming long time ago? Did life circumstances or people close to you crush you from dreaming? In your head, do you hear yourself saying it is impossible, it is absurd, or it is unrealistic? Sometimes, our dreams become heartaches, heartbreaks, and disappointments, and we feel all hope is gone. We're hurt,

LET THERE BE LIGHT

and we're scared to be humiliated by the trials and tribulations that life has brought us. But do not give up on your dream; do not give up on your heart's desire. Identify your dream killers and crush them, avoid them, detour around them, avoid them, and start believing in yourself and in the positivity of yourself and hope.

As you begin to feed on positivity, look at what inspires you to become or to do? As we shape and label the points on the star, yes, luminate; understand there must be a core. The core is what sparkles and glistens for the world to admire. Your heart's desire is being carried out and has left for the world.

Your Reflection Toolkit

1. What is your heart's desire? What are you willing to do to accomplish your desire?
2. What are the steps to get you to that success? Map it out.

CENTER POINT

How to assess motivation factors: personal push points

The center point of Nia is what motivates you, combined with what you envision, the passion you feel, and what gives you satisfaction; you then have found your *sweet spot*.

The center or middle of the star will consist of your heart's desire. Your center point can/will/should/might expand or change as you are exposed to more experiences. For example, you might start off desiring to be a defense attorney, but the desire after law school morphed into a career pursuit as a sports attorney. This new desire may come about because of exposure to sports and contracts. The center point holds the pathway pillar. Remember, the pathway points to the center point to readiness, speed, confidence, motivation, diligence, and know-how. A child may like Legos. Exposure to building blocks and Legos can lead to a desire of engineering architect. Without exposure, the child may grow up only dreaming of becoming a construction worker since construction workers are seen more, and the complexity of an architect is seen less. The new exposure to a bigger frame will result into a bigger vision and a purpose.

Vision

We hear all the time the word *vision*. The meaning gets lost and may be overused or even misused. That does not diminish its importance to the plan, the strategy, or the direction. Vision is what the picture of the destination is. It is like a picture (vision) of that

Hawaiian cruise dream. You can see the islands with you sitting on the beach in your sexiest swimwear. You see yourself walking along the beach sipping on your Hawaiian cold drink, soaking in the beautiful weather. You even feel the black sand (yes, the sand is truly black) flow through your toes. For this to become real, plans must be made and implemented. Flight plans must be reserved. Oh, wait! Money must be available. Clothes must be packed unless new clothes will be purchased on the island. The point we are getting to is this: vision of the vacation trip and the plans for the destination must have plans and tactics carried out. That is the same thing about vision. Look at vision as the biggest, most outlandish destination that you can think.

Steps to the destination should be incredibly challenging. Although huge, the steps need tactics that are achievable a little at a time so that you do not become overwhelmed.

Your vision can be short-term (less than three years) and long-term (five to fifteen years). In my practice, I must do this so I do not get sidetracked. Making goals also helps me identify if I am productive or spinning a hamster wheel. It may not have clarity for you. Conduct an in-depth research on what you like doing. Having a vision in place shifts the direction for growth through exposure or information received.

Let us make it succinct—vision is how you see something holistically. How you see yourself holistically is the definition we will use in this lesson. The way you see yourself in your career may require education certification or work experience. If it does, then the vision must include completion of the requirements. It may consist of learning of particular products and industries.

Purpose

Why are you here? I mean, why are you on earth? Dr. Myles Munroe (2015) challenged his readers to find their purpose for being on earth and living out that purpose. Once you discover your purpose, life becomes so sweet. You will run to those things that fulfills your purpose. You will know when to say "yes" and when to say "no." You will not run to every SOS (shining object syndrome). I found myself running throughout the corporate maze until I found my purpose. I ran through the maze because of someone else's purpose. I saw them flowing, thinking that would give me peace and satisfaction. Wrong! Until I discovered my purpose, I then found peace. Your purpose will come as easy work. So easy that it will not feel like work. Mark Twain says, "Find a job you enjoy doing, and you will never have to work a day in your life." If you can do it for free and feel fulfillment, more than likely, it is your purpose.

Your purpose can be filled in many avenues to get you to your beautiful boulevard. I like to use my pastor, Leon McDonald III, as a model on purpose. His purpose is to coach others to win. He does it on an athletic level by coaching basketball and football. He coaches for his employer by leading a team of employees as a regional district manager. Finally, he coaches the people as pastor on a spiritual level. As I said before, your purpose is utilized on many fronts. So do not think of your purpose in one specific vein. You must think outside the box, and find all the arteries that you purpose flows in.

Here is another example I was fascinated by. I was listening to the Senate's reader during the impeachment trial. The reader reads aloud all the documents to the Senate chamber (cabinet). He is the Senate's reader. That is what he does—read documents aloud. You may enjoy reading.

Do not limit that thought to reading to a room full of kindergartners only. I enjoyed a high school class "Reader's Interpreting," where we took articles and children's stories and made them come alive through voice animation. Wow! That is three modes for reading for one's purpose.

My purpose is teaching and training. I look for different types of teaching opportunities. One way is in the classroom. Another way is one-on-one and even in coaching and, of course, training from this book.

LET THERE BE LIGHT

Your purpose is not for you, it is for society—those here on earth who need you. Your purpose is to expand and grow. The people need what you have. Not walking in your purpose is selfish. The world needs what you have. Until you find your purpose, you will find an emptiness. But then again, when you discover your purpose, oh, how joyful you are in sharing your work with the world. As I think on purpose, I think about legacy.

Your Reflection Toolkit

1. As you reflect on what you see for your life, where are you in one year, five years, or twenty years?
2. You were created for a purpose. Your purpose is unique. Spend time reflecting on what you do well, what you do with ease, and what you could do until the end of the journey.
3. What are your seven core values? These values are not negotiable or compromised. In other words, your purpose cannot be compromised for success.

RAZOR'S EDGE

How to balance being open for change but not losing personal unique gifts (sink or swim)

    A significant point to be aware of with steps toward a vision is to be aware of the *razor's edge* between being authentic and assimilating. So many times, we make attempts to conform what is around us. Remember, I said I wandered around corporate. I worked in some areas because others found pleasure in those jobs, and it made it look easy. Actually, those were good jobs; however, not fit for me. Those coworkers were working in their purpose. I could *not* find comfort or pleasure in those jobs as they did. I did not stay in the position long because I refused to lose myself. I had to be authentic. I had to find the ease of fulfillment, day in and day out. You know what came out of it all? I found me and my purpose—my sweet spot. Others said how they saw me in my purpose. From that, I saw how my authenticity shown in the classroom. My coworkers did not know that I had been terribly miserable, uncomfortable, and unhappy in those previous positions.

LET THERE BE LIGHT

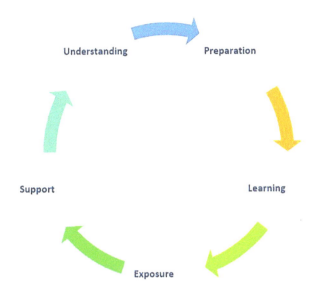

You too can find where the razor's edge is for you. There is a fine line between being unique when working toward goals, social, political, and business environments have the potential to cloud and even diminish one's distinctive traits, gifts, talent, and purpose. Think about this: your social media habits may compromise your beliefs. Our other habits may diminish how you think politically by going along with the masses because of fear of isolation or rejection.

Stand firm on your abilities, your gifts, and talents. Confidence goes a long way because it includes the sharp razor's edge. You need to have confidence, intelligence, emotional, and spiritual stability to walk on that razor's edge. Do you know who you are? Is it coming clearer to you as you move further?

Your Reflection Toolkit

1. Standing on the edge of success, what are you prepared to do for your success?
2. Reflect back on the three pivoting points in your life. What are they? How did they change your beliefs and confidence?

CENTRIFUGAL FORCE: THE SCIENCE OF NIA

How to have sensitivity for timing, pace, and pulse points in life (pacing the speed)

Centrifugal force is the force that is necessary to keep an object moving in a curved path and that is directed inward toward the center of rotation. Theories of a star's brilliance is tied to a centrifugal force, which is movement from the center (the heart's desire). The center of the Nia Star circles around the supporting forces. The center of the star is one's primary pulse point (the heartbeat) to drive energy toward vision, passion, and short/long-term goals.

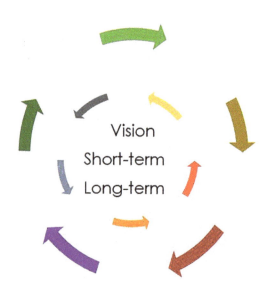

LET THERE BE LIGHT

As the centrifugal force is defined as the apparent force felt by an objective, moving in a curved path outwardly, the force moves away from the center (the frame of reference). The rotation pushes away from the center, even though the inward force is keeping you from going off target. Just wait until we define the five points!

Remember Sir Isaac Newton's first law of motion. It declares that a body at rest will remain at rest, and a body in motion will remain in motion UNLESS it is acted upon by an external force (an experience of inertia). As kids, we have held hands and spun around, picking up a great force, only to let go of hands. Notice how we continued spinning until the momentum slowed us down. If you have spun around on a merry-go-round, you have experienced centripetal and centrifugal force.

Centrifugal force is an inertial force caused by the motion of the frame of reference itself and not by an external force. The realness of your centrifugal force are the five points. Awareness of who is added to the points of the star should be tied to the center, which enables stimulation of the force needed to achieve goals.

In the Nia Star, the centrifugal force represents timing for interactions and alignment of resources and people. To everything, there is a season; that being the case, timing is graciously and respectfully modified or changed as crucial to your success.

Your Reflection Toolkit

1. Set aside a day and time to network. This task may require more than one day in order to list networking events.
2. Set aside a day and time to connect with those who are on the same path or may be helpful to your journey.
3. Establish a cadence for your force.

STAR POINTS

Stars are balls of gas, but we see them as pointed or spiky objects. The star symbol is ubiquitous. Since we all see out of a different lens, which is unique, this would mean that no two people see a star the same way. Our star, the NIA concept, is the star that symbolizes fame—as in the Hollywood Walk of Fame experience, as in five-star generals, or as in a five-star hotel or restaurant.

We see stars more like points of light rather than as larger disk. These stars have some structure to them. Diffraction is one of the clearest examples of lighting behaving like a wave, just like you. For example, light passes through sharp edges, light diffracts and shines. As you travel through life, you travel around narrow openings (to get into a room to sit at the corporate table) or round sharp edges (competing with your competitors); you set off a diffraction pattern, shining and illuminating with your spiritual, physical, emotional, and psychological brilliance. The concept of NIA is that you as a star are structured to shine, diffract, illuminate, and succeed.

There are five points of Nia Star that represent purposeful relationships for interaction to support the pathway to personal goals. The star points provide networking that enhance your skills through a variety of experiences. The Nia Star points have awareness and sensitivity to diversity elements.

A Star

This is not a scientific theory but my metaphonic creation. This book is to help you discover, uncover, and break you through the star

LET THERE BE LIGHT

that is within you. Furthermore, this book is to help you navigate each of the five points' brilliance and usage in shining brightly.

As we look at stars, we cannot help but to see the components of a star's alignment with you. A star is an astronomical object of voluminous, so for it to be one, it has to have plasma, which holds it together by its own gravity. Just the same, you are made up of flesh held together by bones, blood, and muscle. Our bodies stay on earth because it is held down by gravity whereas stars are suspending in the Galaxy by gravity.

A star's life begins with the gravitation collapse of a gassy nebula. For humans, our life begins with ovum's collaboration with sperm cell. This is not to challenge your belief of life before during or after gestation. Nebula is that cloud or fog of dust like embryo, waiting for life to take form. It seems that our star's potential of humans may remain in a nebula form. A star's interior carries every energy away from its core through radiative and convective heat transfer. Let us look at your inner core—the energy.

Just like fuel in a gas tank, it has no bearing just sitting in the gas tank. The energy inside of you has no power left alone in that inner place. A fuel reacts to other substances, such as thought or passion that releases energy. For example, heat movement or working components all makes sense if we are to think of fueling a battery being connected with an appliance. The appliance works because of the fuel released from the battery. We can use another source to convey the same principle. For example: electricity, natural gas, or water.

One must press the accelerator and get the motor revved to put the vehicle in motion. Come on, nebula! Put your foot on the pedal! You will not falter, fail, or collapse. Gravity will hold you up. Yes, your inner power prevents you from a collapsing disaster.

Gravity controls the trajectory of bodies in our solar system and the universe. As a whole, using the law of attraction and magnetism, all matter has weight, which is what holds us down to earth. That is our gravity. Conversely, as we move further from earth into outer space, we lose our weight (those things that hold you down that prevents you from shining) and become weightless suspended by gravity. Stars are weightless and float around the universe, illuminating their brilliance. You, my sister, want to lose your weight that holds you down so you can move around like a star—weightless and possessing the ability that you can, that you will, and that you are able to luminate your purpose.

Your inner core (if you are a person of faith—Holy Spirit) has the fuel, building up in you that energy, which transfers to a desire and passion. That fuel is nothing without you working it to transfer it to something like a thought, a plan, or a goal that needs execution. Making the best of your inner power, Holy Spirit or your higher power, requires you to know yourself. There are many books and assessment tools and resources you may use to learn about yourself. To name a few, we have Myers Briggs Type Indicator (MBTI), DISC Personality Profile, Kirksey, strength Finder, Personality Profile, and KOLBE. I can help you with any one of these. Contact sonya@gtgrowthservices.com.

Look at your inner circle. Is it energizing, stretching you, and growing you? Does it make good deposits into your soul often, or are the people in your inner circle stressing and depressing you? Do they make emotional withdrawal so often you find yourself nonsufficient every time you talk or meet? You must find strength to remove them from your inner circle. Are you in a circle with people who are positive to your soul, they confirm and affirm that your inner energy, Holy Spirit or your higher power, is spoking to your heart?

You also must let your inner power control your physical body. I struggle in this area. I have some health challenges that can (notice I said *can*) be controlled by exercise and diet. Ugh, how I detest writing this passage. Regular exercise and a diet that complement your personal health challenge is the only way to live and let your inner power release the energy—luminating the Nia Star's power of full brilliance.

Connecting with the source of your power is a true path to gain your inner power in your inner core. It does not matter what your spiritual source is. Whatever, whomever it is, establish and increase your connectivity through prayer, meditation, and studying which is a way to center yourself—to your spiritual source, the universe, and the people within it.

LET THERE BE LIGHT

Anchor

How to identify that best friend who can be trusted

An anchor is a reliable or principal support. Your anchor holds you firmly in your beliefs, your dreams, your values, and your inspiration. The fact of the matter, your anchor *knows* you. Knowing you inside and out, though thick and thin, your anchor has an *agape* love for you (unconditional). In every aspect of your life, your anchor is there—good and bad, celebrations and sorrow.

For sanity's sake, your anchor not only understands you, but celebrates with you and for you. Can you imagine going through life's journey without an anchor? Can you imagine not being sharpened by someone you trust? What I mean here is *iron sharpens iron*, according to Proverbs 27:17—someone who can tell you when you are off, wrong, or need clarity. That is what an anchor does.

Let us get a bit more clarity of an anchor. Have you needed to vent? Call your anchor. Do you need to cry? Call your anchor. Is your character coming into question? Your anchor may defend you. Yes, an anchor is that reliable support you can depend on. Even so, did you just get a new job or promotion? You know you must call your anchor.

When I look back on my life, I realize I have two anchors. How blessed is that! There is Pat and Deborah. They have anchored me since fourth grade (age nine). That is over fifty years of supporting me. Of course, I support them. Guess what? Pat and Deborah have journeyed with me in all but two phases of my life—infancy and toddler years. We've been there for all the celebratory times as well as disappointments. I know Pat, and she knows me. I know Deborah, and she knows me too. We labeled ourselves as "G" girls since our last names begin with the letter G. Today, we do not call one another friends. We say we are sisters—sisters with a strong bond anchored in friendship, anchored in spirit, anchored in love, and anchored in sisterhood.

The body goes through changing phases at different stages of life. Think about it, these stages of my life included Pat and Deborah. Although we met in the last part of our childhood, we played hopscotch, jump rope, and bat and ball to name a few. Puberty, from nine to thirteen, brought us as Girl Scouts to becoming into womanhood, to self-discoveries, and the Jackson Five. Adolescence (fourteen to eighteen) made us aware of boys and hobbies (more self-discoveries), especially how to win at school academically (courses, exams, and college acceptance), socially (prom and afterschool activities), and athletically (dance team, volleyball). Then we got to adulthood. Oh my, this was the time we KNEW we had made it. Adulthood stretches from nineteen through middle age. We experienced being roommates, experienced marriages, attending and dropping out of college, finding our first employment, motherhood, our first car, and everything in between. There were some disappointments with life during our adulthood (divorces, miscarriages, and some death). We were there for one another, supporting with laughter and tears.

We made it through middle age (thirty-one to fifty years of age). We realize that we had carried out a life of responsibility and accountability. We have watched each of us raise children, hold down careers, stay in faith, and maintain our femininity.

Now, here we are in our senior years, the years until the end. Now, we experience grandchildren and retirement. My goodness, as I write this, I reminisce of each of those stages with my anchors. The last disappointment I had, both Pat and Deborah reminded me of who I am and how I am made up. I can expect the truth. Such honesty helps in development. Anchors allow you to be your true self because your anchor knows your flaws, your weaknesses, and your idiosyncrasies.

As much as Pat and Deborah witnessed and experienced many of life changes with me, our love for one another has never faded. As we ventured through adulthood (marriage, divorce, children, and careers), our visits or telephone conversations were no longer every day or long. As a matter a fact, our talks were separated by four to five months apart. But guess what? We could not tell the difference of every day talks or five-month conversations. Our talks continued from the last time without missing a beat. There is respect and support of motherhood, wifehood, and career-building that requires time and energy. We respected each other's role.

An anchor does not have to be with you 24-7, think or act like you, or agree with you on everything. However, your core values are aligned though. Respect is a true characteristic of the relationship. Disagreements are shared with love and never cavalier or cause a fall out. An anchor tells you want you NEED to hear despite what you WANT to hear. That person is the voice of reason. An anchor wants to see you get better. That person feels your pains but, as stated before, shares your joys and celebrates with you. An anchor is someone you share good and bad memories with. An anchor is cherished and is hard to come by and difficult to leave and impossible to forget. The anchor is the first person you think about "What would (my anchor) think?

Your anchor might be a sister or mother—someone who has known you most all your life. The relationship has the same characteristics: TRUST, VALUE, HONESTY, LOVE, and RESPECT.

Now, answer this. Who knows your quirks, your oddities, and your individualism? Is it your mother, your father, your sister, or your best friend? Who? Who anchors who you are, or even who you are not? Next to God, or your Supreme Being, who on earth holds you firmly and anchors you? We were put on earth for each other. You need an anchor. I thank God for Pat Green Davis and Deborah Gayles-Hill, who are my anchors and who continue loving and supporting me today. They are my anchors—my two sisters.

Peer

How to bond with someone on the same platform, who can be trusted and is encouraging

We could use the word associate, companion, crony, compeer, or comrade. But a peer in this sense is a person of the same status and ability. We could use *colleague* since the term can be used as one who bands for the same cause.

As the second point of the NIA, your peer or colleague are in the struggle with you. This person knows all that it takes to cross the finish line. But unlike the anchor, the peer may not know your flaws. There is a limitation. As a matter a fact, they know you based on what you have in common. However, the peer shares many of your values. As your journeying through to accomplish your goals, so is your peer. Your peer is also looking for the beautiful boulevard.

Unlike your anchor, you are able to bounce ideas with your peer since you may be working on the same thing (i.e., math class, law school, work projects). Your anchor may be working toward different goals, and thus, do not understand the challenges you are dealing with. Albeit, your peer is right in the fight and feels all the pains and struggles you are feeling and experiencing.

Through my education, I developed peers who worked on similar assignments with me. It would be totally unfair to think that I could have done this alone and by myself. Eloquently stated by John Maxwell, "One is too small a number to achieve greatness" (2001). No one has made success by oneself. Tiger Wood had a caddie, a golf coach, and even his equipment—tailor-made golf clubs to fit and ensure his swing and style can make the difference for Tiger's expertise in golfing. Each of these people/company is an attribute to Tiger winning. That is the same for you and your peer. You may study together. You need each other. You may share nuggets of wisdom that helps you both achieve your goals. Your relationship may grow beyond your struggle. It can grow deeper and last for years.

LET THERE BE LIGHT

Mentor

How to approach and secure a mentor supporting your life's vision, who can be trusted, and is encouraging

Mentors are those who help you in your personal and professional development. Instead of making mistakes and taking the long way, a mentor will guide you in avoidance of mistakes, and most importantly, navigate you around obstacles. Those obstacles may have been lessons learned that the mentor experienced. Some organizations have mentorship programs, where mentors are assigned to mentees based on profiles and career fields. In a mentorship relationship, there are advantages for both parties, which makes opportunities for powerful win/wins. Do not force a mentorship relationship. Intentionality is good except in finding a mentor. The best approach is to build relationships with people and learn from them. As you build relationships, a mentor will/may see you out. Mentorship relationships can start organically, where it just happens authentically.

Usually, a mentor is an expert in your desired field. However, your mentor may be an expert in another field but has expertise that can guide and advise you. Your mentor provides you with tools, guidance, support, and feedback, which you need to thrive and grow and advance in your career. Your mentor can be a family, friend, alumnus, coworker, current/former boss, or even someone you connected with through networking. The mentor should have gone down the road you are on. You mentor has blazed the trail and knows and understands the landscape. Do you think it would not be painful to learn from errors someone else has made?

Your mentor should be close at hand. You cannot just admire the mentor from afar, which is why celebrities are not your mentor or role model. Remember, this is a relationship. You have to have a developing relationship. Show and tell your mentor what you are doing. Do not expect your mentor to arbitrary tell you and, especially. show you. You must ask and show forward-thinking. Forward-thinking shows you have initiative for your own growth and development.

Are you tired of being stuck? Your mentor can help you get unstuck if you are struggling in any aspects of your work. Case in point, while working as a supervisor, my subordinates were huddled together talking. I inquired about the topic only to discover they were talking about the manager (my leader), and how disgusted they felt because he would touch them and stand over them, invading their personal space. Initially, I laughed and said, "Oh, you know how he is." I walked back to my desk. Once there, I quickly reflected, "I am an ambassador for the company, I am to reduce or eliminate liability. MY GOSH, I have to report this or talk to someone.

I began writing a memo to my boss's boss. But before I could hit send, I felt a pulling in my stomach. *Wait! Call HR.* I could not reach the HR consultant. Feeling an anxiety overcoming me, I called on my mentor. After he laughed, he said, "Sonya, don't send his boss that email. Have a conversation with your boss. Give him an opportunity to make corrections on his behavior. Let him know that if you hear this again, you will have no recourse but to report it." I said all this to emphasize how a good mentor will help you through any of your struggles.

Look for a mentor who is enthusiastic about his/her own expertise. The enthusiasm he/she exhibits is partly what excites you. Actually, he/she makes it appear easy. A mentor is enthusiastic about your journey and accomplishments. But he/she should NOT be more enthusiastic as you are. If you are NOT fired up, your mentor will help you build your confidence. Your confidence is what fuels and excites you. During the time, your mentor shows more enthusiasm than the mentee, so be assured that the mentor is working to affirm what he/she sees deep inside of you. The mentor's assignment is to bring that which is uncovered within you to the forefront of your potential, basically uncovering the best you have. Your mentor should be a difference-maker for your personal and professional development. A good mentor will create strategies that stretch you without breaking you. For growth, you will undergo areas of pain. This is aligning with the Law of the Rubber Band and the Law of Pain (Maxwell 2012).

LET THERE BE LIGHT

Your mentor has a philia (friendship or brotherly love) love for you. It is imbuing with respect, constructive feedback, and compassion. Do not get me wrong, a mentor may have to discipline you. Understand that is done in private (quite naturally) and is conducted before praising you (my concept of praise and polish).

Praise and polish is to provide feedback while the person receiving the feedback only listens, to not say anything except "thank you" for what you did good (praise) and what you can improve upon (polish). You can take it in or spit it out if you do not agree. At no time do you make excuses or justifications. As a mentee, you may notice that the praise and polish episode may have solutions. Do not become defensive. Your mentor has your success in his/her heart to maintain and grow you professionally. If you do not believe he/she does not, consider leaving the mentorship relationship.

Do you not want to be called out on your fallacies? Why are you unresponsive and defensive to being polished? Do not shy away from constructive feedback. You know you did not learn how to do math without some failure before you succeed at it.

The stretching is a trigger for encouragement. If you stay in your comfort zone, you will not get you to where you desire. Growth requires stretching. I remember this young boy in church named Robert. Robert would spend the summers with his dad in California. He grew six inches each summer. It was obvious: he was going to be tall. During the school year, he complained of knee and shin pain. Mom took him to the pediatrician for X-rays. It was discovered that he had gaps in his knee joints. Why? Because he had a destiny to be tall. Today, Robert is six feet seven inches. He was being stretched to accommodate the height potential he was to become. If you asked Robert today, he could tell you how painful it was to reach today's height. That is exactly what your mentor is doing for you—stretching you.

While working with a mentor, you should have expectations where the mentor-mentee relationship is going. Since mentors should be life-long learners themselves, he/she is taking you to a higher level as they are on a higher path as well. That is why your success is important to him/her. Through the relationship, do not be surprised if the mentor learns something from you, the mentee. Afterall, the mentor is an expert but does not know everything. So do not be alarmed if your mentor says "I don't know." The upside is the mentor will find the answer. Believe it or not, this is a worthwhile person to continue a mentor-mentee relationship.

Listening is a major key characteristic of your mentor. Mentor must be good listeners and good inquirers too. They are interested in you and where you are going. So much so, he/she removes distractions while meeting with you (not taking phone calls, text messages, and even closing the door so others may not walk in the room). You should exercise reflective listening when your mentor is advising you. Your mentor may ask thought-provoking questions to ascertain what your perspective is and where you are coming from.

Another characteristic to look for in a mentorship relationship is giving and receiving feedback. Since you understand how your success is important to your mentor, you must have respect and trust in what the mentor says and advises. If you have no trust or respect for the mentor, the relationship will NOT yield the expected outcome and should be dissolved.

Watch how your mentor interact with others. His/her emotional intelligence (EI) is the consciousness of one's own emotions, with the ability to make decisions and influence others while controlling emotions but maintaining feelings of empathy.

Your mentor should not have a personal agenda but an objective that is mentee-centered. Whenever you hear the mentor ask, "What do you think you should do?" Understand the challenge and the role the mentor respects and expects of you—to have control of yourself. At no time should the mentor take the reins of your independence. While we are here, be mindful of duplicating or mirroring your mentor. Your experience and journey will look different, and it should. Your success (however you define it) should feel right to you and follow your beliefs and values. That is not saying your beliefs and values do not align with your mentor. Quite frankly, it does; however, your perspective lens is different. Instead, you are to keep your authentic self but use the resources and tools to improve the true you. You are aspiring to have his/her skills and NOT becoming him/her when you grow up.

Stay true to yourself, and do what feels right for you. Stay focus on your core values and beliefs. Do not stray away because of your mentor. Be true to yourself, and be authentic always.

It is okay to have more than one mentor. Each mentor has a specific focus and should know when to lob the ball to someone else when something is outside of the realm of expertise. I recall a mentor-mentee relationship I had. The mentee needed a second mentor, so I recommended a fellow employee. He was always excited and enthused about his next project. On the contrary, she did not agree with his ideology. After she shared what she meant, I explained that was exactly what she needed for her growth—someone who thought differently. If she only connected with people who thought as she, she could not/would not expand. She accepted and made the connection. She requested his service to mentor her. She really appreciated his mentorship. Furthermore, he was so honored and excited to mentor her.

Just as you need a mentor, it is just as important for you to become one. Being a mentor develops your leadership skills for you experiencing new opportunities of meeting new people.

Remember that as you give you give back. You, too, can be a mentor to someone up and coming. Do not horde the information. I like to say it this way: Knowledge is not knowledge unless it is shared. Helping someone develop, grow, and navigate life is fulfilling and has dividends. Mentoring challenges you to depths you cannot imagine.

Sponsorship

How to manage relationships with someone on a level who can make a difference

A sponsor is someone who supplies and support you emotionally, financially, intellectually, vocationally. The sponsor gives assurance.

We have heard the term *sponsor* when the discussion is on advertisement of some sort. Perhaps, taking a line from this prism, a sponsor guides one through because they have walked that path and knows the triggers that the protégé may encounter. The protégé may ask questions and offer accountability. As one moves through the issues, the sponsor has an understanding posits while giving love confidentiality. Confidentiality is crucial to the relationship.

According to the definition, the sponsor-protégé relationship success is based on honesty and objectivity, with trust and respect not far behind. Having or being a business (corporate) sponsor is about advertising or marketing (branding) that supports an individual. You may wonder how this relates to your star point.

As you look for a sponsor, he/she may look to the protégé to build his/her brand whilst assisting to climbing the ladder of success.

Sponsors advocate actively for you behind closed doors and publicly, politically, and creditably to get you access to opportunities or titles/roles that you would not have access to on your own. A sponsor is NOT a one-size-fits-all. The sponsor is carefully and selectively chosen. Understand that the sponsor's name goes on the protégé's brand. This is why the sponsor is strategic on putting the sponsor's name out there as to who to connect with. Their finances and career are dependent on the protégé's success.

Look at how Nike aligns who they are to a reputable athlete. If, however, the protégé does not live up to Nike's brand, Nike severances the relationship. We have seen this countless times of a sponsor having to severance relationships because of proprietaries. Just the same, while looking for and connecting with a prospective protégé, the sponsor looks at how your values align with theirs. As a matter a fact, the sponsor is looking at how you align to his/her values. It is a two-way relationship.

According to Jo Miller, mentors help you *skill up* whereas sponsors help you *move up*. A mentor talks to you, but a sponsor talks about you. And hear this, a mentor shows you the ropes. Guess what? A sponsor helps you climb the ropes. A good read is Miller's book *Woman of Influence: 9 Steps to Build Your Brand, Establish Your Legacy, and Thrive* (2020), where there is great understanding of how women have been over-mentored yet under-sponsored relative to men.

Champion

How to manage relationships with someone on a higher level who can open doors for goals

When we hear the term champion, how quickly we think about athletics and teams being the proven best in the particular genre. This point of the Nia Star is that the champion is a person who volunteers to help you adapt and implement your success—usually a policy, program, project, or product.

A champion creates an influential synergetic factor in achieving a major purpose for the organization. The champions sustain, nurtures, and transform your growth. This growth comes by way because a champion has ten strong characteristics (Porter Lynch 2012):

1. Visionary
2. Energetic
3. Confident (can-do attitude)
4. Team player
5. Focus, with strong beliefs
6. Charismatic
7. Risk-taker
8. Innovative and creative
9. Tenacious and perseverant
10. Seeks opportunity

A good champion will visualize your growth and potential. She envisions where you can go—your possibilities. You may not see your potential, but your champion can.

Looking at your potential, you should be fueled by your passion. However, your champion sees the potential with such enthusiasm that you would think it is her dream. Fueling the enthusiasm keeps the champion energized. The vision is so big she runs after what is desired. It may seem like the champion goes without sleep.

Another characteristic of a champion is a can-do spirit. The champion's confidence is very high. It is almost like the champion has a cape and is transformed to superwoman. Because of this can-do attitude, the champion has sought to work with you—you show a can-do spirit as well (Miller 2016). After all, your champion wants to see you improve and become your best you. Don't you want that for yourself? That can-do attitude translates to hard work, dedication, and learning from mistakes.

We discussed earlier about not working in a silo; well, here we go again. Your champion is a team player and works diligently in helping you become an outstanding team player. It may feel like corporate politics at times. if corporate bothers you, you may have to get out of your comfort zone. It is not going away. Does it feel like a stretching? Of course, it does. Because your champion wants you to grow and succeed. Champions do not hold back. They give their all in the littlest things and focus for the greater good of the team.

While you may want to connect with the champion, bear in mind that *charisma* is vital. He or she advocates and promotes you for you. If no one listens or support your champion, you have to ask yourself, *Is he or she truly a champion other than in title?* When others know who your champion is, doors and opportunities will open for you. Are you confident enough to walk through those doors?

The other side of the door are splendid opportunities for waiting for you to leap. Leaping at any splendid opportunity is a challenge and requires risk-taking. Knowing that your champion has your best interests and is there to even coach you. Your time being coached may involve innovative discoveries. I like the fact that my champion gave me the idea and let me go at it. I was empowered to create database, presentations, an agenda for leadership meetings. He gave me autonomy because he championed my growth and creativity. I never felt stifled. I enjoyed each challenge he presented.

It has been said "losers never win, and winners never quit." Your champion is just that tenacious and perseverant. Those two qualities should be seen in you. Understand that your champion is advocating to put you in front of an audience you would not normally get.

Therefore, quitting when you fall or fatigue is NEVER an option. Every day is another opportunity to funnel through. Being the champion is not a mediocre feat; connecting with a champion purely means not being average, not accepting mediocracy but improving daily.

These five points of NIA means you are teachable and coachable; the champion is no different. The champion removes areas that could block you from walking through the door and getting on that stage. Now, do not go off thinking that having a champion is going to make your quest for your success easy. Having a champion takes a lot of the challenging barriers down. You still must do the work period. You must work your plan. You must be up for the challenge. All the work is for you to reach your heart's desire.

If you are weak in a particular area, your champion will point it out to you by having you register for training, etc. My champion handed me the corporate training catalog, telling me to schedule for any and all courses I desire to take that would grow and strengthen me. Never had I been given carte blanche for training period. He was serious about taking me upward.

There may be an encounter that resources are scarce or absent. Your champion will seek out the necessary tools and dollars for you, almost like having his or her skin in the game period. Why? Champions feel the pain and perhaps felt them on his or her journey. Women and minorities are less likely to have a sponsor and, especially, a champion, which is why the glass ceiling, an invent-invisible barrier, is very challenging to break and rises above certain level of hierarchies and C-suites.

Working with the champion may come with barriers also. If you are not up for a rigorous schedule, do not engage until you are ready. Champions may experience complexities to help you change or breakthrough time constraints, priorities, work schedules, and assignments. A lack of clarity and unclear expectations, along with a lack of leadership and management support, are examples of barriers. A champion's expertise allows him or her to funnel through the barriers; after all, a champion is energized, tenacious, and perseverant. Now, can you partner with him or her? The reward is awesome.

Do not just be a champion; join the ranks of paying it forward—be a champion. A champion may not be in a C-suite or executive position. As a champion, you plan, practice, and prepare for the big moment. Can you do that? Consider how you can help make others around you better. Championing a woman can be fulfilling. Be the cheerleader for her. Be at the table for her, encourage her and her ideas and insights. As you climb, lift! The illumination of your star shines even more brilliantly. Clusters of brilliant stars shine even more brilliant.

Herrick (2017) suggests that women support one another in the conference room, period. She contents that women sit in the front and center, encouraging accomplishments of other women and providing positive direct feedback. Sponsorship and mentorship are two of the best ways to develop leadership and reach back at the same time. Champion is included and has the best payoff—a great return.

Your Reflection Toolkit

1. Identify each of your points. Who is the anchor, peer, mentor, sponsor, and champion?
2. If you do not have anyone on the star, make a list of potential people to seek.
3. Schedule with those in the above list. As you have a developed relationship, inquire about how they can benefit as a point on your Nia Star.

DISTRACTIONS

How many times have you begun an arduous task and got deep into it, only to get distracted? Or before you begin, you succumb to distractions? Those distractions can be opening emails, scrolling social media, or even taking phone calls. However, distractions come. Those distractions take you away from your focus—they take you away from your goals. Jesus said to his disciples, "Things that cause people to stumble are bound to come, but woe to anyone for whom they come" (Luke 17:1 NIV). So knowing that we cannot eradicate distractions while on our journey, we have to find ways around and through them.

Distractions are a form of a stumbling block. Stumbling blocks indicate a circumstance that causes difficulty or hesitation. Is that not like a distraction? We may hesitate because we are attempting to be perfect or complete a task with perfections—flawless. We are regretting yesterday's missteps, or we are so focused on tomorrow. Yes, we have a desire to have everything right. Yet having it right does not preclude excellence.

So we asked, is distraction a curse or blessing? Not doing what we should can cause us to miss deadlines, fail in classes, or crash into other drivers. In this case, distractions are a curse because these kinds of distractions pull us away from what is more important. Distractions can make us better. They can help us cope with the pains of everyday life. That is when you are so engrossed in what you are doing that you're not paying attention to that which is around you. For example, if you are a mother with a toddler, you are so engrossed in what you are doing that you are not paying attention to what the child is doing. That can be harmful or even fatal to the child. That is

LET THERE BE LIGHT

why some distractions, like this kind of distraction, is not a blessing. Even when you cannot hear your child playing, as my mother would say, this could mean that the child is getting into destruction. Or the child is getting into something, and suddenly, you hear screaming because the child has gotten into something. Have you ever thought about the child getting into the cabinet where the bleach is kept? You can hear the cabinet opening if you're not distracted.

Our brains have a limited ability to focus, which means we have to train our brain to focus. So I would say, you have to choose what you will focus on. Use self-regulation tactics to help you avoid distraction. Be aware of and control your behaviors and your thoughts. How do you do that? Make sure you get enough sleep. For example, I found it bad sitting up late although I am not sleepy. This causes me to get up late or to be distracted in my thought processes during the day. I had to train my body and my mind that I must go to sleep at a certain hour to get a full night's rest.

Distractions can be a good thing or what we call a blessing. Everyone deals with distractions. Although they seem to pull us away from important things, distractions do serve a purpose. Distractions can help us cope with the pains of everyday life. They can help us to stay fit, such as being distracted with music or television may improve performance and endurance. I found this to be very helpful for me while working. I would go so deep into my thoughts while writing a training material. I like to work around a little bit of noise. I can hear things around me but as I hear the noises, my mind is continuously thinking. It is almost like white noise. As I need to take a short break, the noise around me was tuned up louder. It allows my brain to rest so I can go back even stronger in my thought processes.

Research has shown that even puzzle games like Candy Crush or Word Search puzzles might help us with our distraction which keeping us from even eating ice cream. So what is your reason for your distraction? Digital games are powerful tools to best build strength and confidence, but attempting to overcome these challenges within a game, you should not find yourself avoiding work. These kinds of distractions pull us away from our priorities, so we may find that we are having trouble limiting our use of Candy Crush. I am guilty of that one because I discovered it sucks me right in. I discovered that Facebook scrolling was a time-stealer for me as well. I now time my Facebook usage unless I am on a Facebook live webinar or worship service.

Author Dr. Jane McGonigal suggests that you look at why you are engaged in a distraction. Are your favorite digital distractions being used as a tool to build strength, skills, knowledge, and self-efficacy? Or are they temporary escapes from an uncomfortable reality? Are you regretting your yesterday? Call your mistake just what it is—a mistake. Move on, and learn from it. Are you experiencing distractions because you are trying to "keep up with the Joneses" or today, it is "keeping up with the Kardashians." You are focusing on the wrong Bing, and it's draining your energy. Do not let the distractions of what's happening around you through other people cause you to mess your opportunities that are before you.

The hardest distraction to avoid are the internal distractions. Internal distractions our thoughts and emotions. This includes thoughts about pressing responsibilities, pleasant things that you wish you were doing, and even things that you have failed at yesterday. We can even include fears and worries. Self-regulation is when you use process to be aware of and to control your behaviors and thoughts. Seek out ways that you can use learning strategies. I'm on self-regulated learning. There are ways to overcome internal distractions. Really, you managed it.

First, schedule time for each task that you have to do. I schedule my week one Sunday by planning my work for the week. I schedule things into half-hour increments. Some things I may schedule for two hours. Afterward, I give myself a break.

Secondly, discover the best time of day that you work on challenging things best. Are you a morning person? Are you one that's very creative and focused on midday? Find your sweet spot of the day. That is the time of day when you should be doing the most challenging and daunting task.

LET THERE BE LIGHT

Thirdly, incorporate fun in your task. How can you make it enjoyable when you know it is that task you least like to do? Give yourself a treat when you complete little segments of the task. The old adage is true: How do you eat an elephant? One bite at a time. Therefore, after a few bites, reward yourself. Another way to avoid distractions is to Write yourself a note if you get distracted. Do not think that because you are on an assignment, you will not get distracted. Our brain is always thinking. Jot down whatever it is that came up in your mind—if it is a word, if it is a sentence, or if it is something you need to research later.

Ask yourself this question, Why do I need to focus? Focus on two or three things that are your important task. Have a dedicated work section. I have been using this system for many years and didn't know that it had a name: *Pomodoro method*. Pomodoro method is amazingly simple. It allows you to take twenty minutes of a task, move to another task, and after one hour or an hour and a half, you take a break for only about five minutes. Then you go back to another task for twenty minutes and another, then take a fifteen-minute break. You can easily stay focus for twenty minutes.

When you are ready to embark on a challenging task, be sure to have water right at your fingertips. Perhaps you need some snacks. Setting these two things at your fingertips can reduce you becoming dehydrated or hungry.

Our world is full of distractions. The most dangerous are those we do not recognize. Some distractors are obvious. Recognize what your distractors are. You would be surprised to find that one thing you did not realize distracts you.

Distractions can help us with the pains of everyday life.

Your Reflection Toolkit

1. What are those things that distract you from doing what you need to do?
2. How do you overcome distractions?

3. What tool do you use to ensure you stay focus and on a task? Describe how it works.
4. Work on tasks for a week using the Pomodoro method. How can you stay focused using this method? What other method can you use to stay on a task with little to no distractions?

GIVE AND RECEIVE

How to share to share knowledge and experiences

There is so much to gain from each star point. True value is the sustainability for being open to give back where one receives. Today, we call it *pay it forward*. Learning and growing are an evolutionary process that requires the balance of exchange. I always say "knowledge is not knowledge unless it's shared." No point on the star has any value if there is not a give and a receive posture.

Awareness of yourself lends itself that you never know when you are needed for another point of the Nia Star. It is possible that the person that is a peer today can be a champion in the future. So give your best always!

As a giver, you are freely and you cherish passing on insight and wisdom and even a point of view. Give from a place of humility and unpretentious posture since the receiver of your giving is often seen as a passive consumption. As a giver, you are in fact providing an opinion that is fact-based. You are in a seat of a giver because, like we said before, "knowledge is not knowledge unless it's shared."

Be sure your emotions are not on display while giving. Well, the emotion you should show is pleasantness—pleased that you have the opportunity to share. Just remember, the receiver is an adult (if they're over eighteen) and can make his or her own decisions. You know how you feel in those shoes. When you look out of your lens, you see from a world view. The view of your experiences, allowing someone to give to you, share experiences, and insight is an opportunity to see from someone else's lenses. You know your limitations and inferences most of the time, so another point of view can be deemed helpful. Do not shun or dismiss it. You may have to let the information marinate. This allows you time to extrapolate the pros and cons, the logic, the rationale for you to make a decision—the best decision.

It may seem easy to give; however, there are barriers that may come about in the expected outcome. For example, if you go to a like-minded cohort, he or she may not be the best avenue to receive since there may be similar viewpoints. Here is when you must have clear values. Allowing a different viewpoint gives you a perspective you or a friend of the same perspective would not have thought about.

You also may have a barrier in place by discounting the giver. If this is the case, ask yourself, *Why don't I trust this person?* If you are the giver, ask, *Why am I being undervalued and dismissed?* It may be your approach, your tone, or your attitude while giving. If this is the case, know it, acknowledge it, accept it, and adjust to it. I call this the three As to gaining knowledge. One thing to keep in mind is that we as humans tend to put more stock in our own opinion even when we lack expertise and have no knowledge on a topic. We were born with a blank slate—all of us. There is so much knowledge out there we cannot get it all. Only God is all-knowing, as in omniscient.

Most receivers misjudge the quality of advice a giver provides. Studies have shown that receivers dismiss, undervalue, and misjudge the giver's advice when it does not agree with the receiver. At the same token, do not give for self-centered motives or being self-serving.

If you are not open and transparent to communicate the entire problem, you do not trust the giver. However, do not overwhelm the giver with too much information. Be careful not to cause the giver the winnow through the cluster of issues.

The final decision is always on the receiver. As stated before, give him or her the respect to do that. Do not get offended with the decision that is not one you provided. In most cases, the receiver may seek more than one giver and may weigh out or combine the options. It is your right to choose and make your decision as the receiver. Here

LET THERE BE LIGHT

is a big *however*: YOU MUST TAKE OWNERSHIP, ACCOUNTABILITY, AND LIVE WITH YOUR DECISION.

Do not take stock in WIIFM—"What's in it for me?"—which can cause you to stumble; and as you journey on the path that you are on, you will develop dead ends—dead ends that lead nowhere because the knowledge, skills, and the experiences were not passed on. That is the fun part about knowledge. As we pass it on, it grows bigger. As we pass it on, it gets wider. As we pass it on, it just morphs into what we see today.

If we think about the technology yesterday with telephones, who would ever think that Alexander Graham Bell, with his can and string, could expand into today's telephones in 2021—with cell phones being powered by satellites and batteries? So do not dismiss what you have to pass on as unvalued or unworthy, or if you think, *You got yours, let him/her figure it out. I got mine.* If you are trying to keep it to yourself, dismiss that. Pass your knowledge on, pass your experiences on, pass your skills on, and you will find yourself growing even larger than where you thought you would be. In the system of life, help makes life easier for the next person.

I remember a story where a man talked about a piece of paper being held down. The wind was blowing strongly. He said he had to run to catch the paper. He held it down with his foot as the wind blew. To keep the paper down, he had to keep his foot on it. Not only is the paper going nowhere, but he could not go anywhere either. So when you hold yourself down to hold that piece of paper in one place, you are holding knowledge down, you are actually holding yourself down. Let it go! Free yourself. Let there be light! Let Nia's brilliance shine brightly. Now, luminate. Let there be light!

Your Reflection Toolkit

1. Remember, knowledge is not knowledge unless it is shared. Now, identify who you will give to. You should have identified those who are points on your Nia Star.

2. Seek out an organization where you can support not only financially, but also in the skills and talents you have.
3. Show gratitude. Send thank-you cards and notes to those who have poured into your life (big or small).

REFERENCES

Bandura, A. 1993. "Self-Efficacy: Toward a Unifying Theory of Behavior." *Psychology Review* 84: 191–215.

Campbell, L., B. Campbell, and D. Dickinson. 2004. *Theory and Development of Multiple Intelligences.* Boston, MA: Allyn & Bacon.

Gardner, H. 1995. "Are There Additional Intelligences? The Case for the Naturalist Intelligence." Harvard Project Zero. Cambridge, MA: President and Fellows of Harvard College.

Gardner, H. 1999. *Intelligence Reframed: Multiple Intelligences for the 21st Century.* New York, NY: Basic Books.

Herrick, L. 2017. *6 Ways to Champion and Empower Other Women Every Day.*

Kelly, B. D. 2014. "A Champion Is More Than an Athlete with a Ring." www.kmco.com.

Krathwohl, D. R. 2002. "A Revision of Bloom's Taxonomy: An Overview." *Theory into Practice* 41 (4): 212–218.

McGonigal, J. 2015. *SuperBetter: The Power of Living Gamefully.* New York, NY: Penguin Random House Books, LLC.

Maslow, A. H. 1943. *A Theory of Human Motivation.* Daryaganj, New Delhi: General Press.

Maxwell, J. C. 2012. *The 15 Invaluable Laws of Growth: Live Them and Reach Your Potential.* New York, NY: Hachette Book Group, Inc.

Maxwell, J. C. 2001. *The 17 Indisputable Laws of Teams: Embrace Them and Empower Your Team.* Nashville, TN: Thomas Nelson, Inc.

Merriam-Webster. 2020.

Miller, J. 2020. *Woman of Influence: 9 Steps to Build Your Brand, Establish Your Legacy, and Thrive.* New York, NY: McGraw-Hill Education.

ABOUT THE AUTHOR

Sonya Carol Thomas is a native of Detroit, Michigan. Her writing explores the many roads traveled to end up successful, seasonal, and sensational. Her book focuses on positive morals and uplifting themes of a directive life well lived. With a PhD in education (post-secondary and adult education), she has a passion for literacy and education, as shown through her teaching assignments at two universities. Although retired from one aspect of the workforce after thirty-eight years, Sonya has not retired completely—she has just decided to finally enjoy the view. She travels widely and enjoys crocheting, pleasure reading, motivating others in coaching and developing leadership and personal development.

She lives with her caring husband, Richard, in Auburn Hills, Michigan.

CPSIA information can be obtained
at www.ICGtesting.com
Printed in the USA
JSHW011558280622
27569JS00004B/12